<u>Once you LOVE this book, which I know you will, please do 3 things for me.</u>

1. Take a selfie of you with the book and post it on Social Media and tag @Delatorro.

2. Leave us an Amazon Review even though you didn't buy it on Amazon.

3. Do a Facebook Live about your Top 3 insights from your book and tell your tribe to get their copy at www.PlatinumPresentationsBook.com.

Thanks in Advance and Congrats on Delivering Platinum Presentations

Delatorro

DELATORRO L. MCNEAL II, MS, CSP

PLATINUM
PRESENTATIONS

52 TIPS

TO SPEAK WITH CONFIDENCE, WIN YOUR AUDIENCE & GROW YOUR BANK ACCOUNT

FOREWORD BY THE LEGENDARY LES BROWN

www.PlatinumPresentations.com
8553 N. Beach St. Suite #298
Fort Worth, TX 76244
Email: Delatorro@gmail.com Website: Delatorro.com
ISBN-13: 978-1985237230
ISBN-10: 1985237237

To order copies of this book in bulk for book clubs, NSA Chapters, Toastmasters Clubs/Districts, community meetings, company staff, professional association membership, church study groups, employee moral & reward programs or non-profit fundraisers, please call (813) 963-5356 for special bulk book pricing.
Printed in the United States.
Cover Design by Scher
Editing & Book Design by Trish Lewis

Online Resources by Delatorro:

www.Delatorro.com

www.CrushTheStageLive.com

www.ToastmasterToTopSpeaker.com

www.TheKeynoteTV.com

www.FullThrottleExperience.com

www.Anointed4Business.com

www.CrushTheStageUniversity.com

www.CrushUniversity.com

Dedication

I also dedicate this book to every orator, communicator, educator and person of excellence who is attracted to it. May this book and the wisdom it contains help you bring the best out of yourself, your presentations and your audiences for many years to come.

Table of Contents

Introduction

In 2017 Warren Buffet officially went on record to say that his Public Speaking course was the most important business class he ever took. He went on to encourage all of his top business student to enroll in Toastmasters International to further polish and develop their skills. Wow...So the wealthiest man in the world attributes his business success to his ability to communicate well. That's amazing. Just think about that for a minute or two...

Empowered Greetings friend. It's Delatorro and I'm so excited that you have this profound book in your personal possession. Just the mere fact that you have attracted this book into your life whether by purchasing it for yourself or someone giving it to you as a gift - the fact that you have it and are reading it tells me a lot about you.

You are a high achiever. You are a peak performer. You are a powerful soul and a necessary voice in this world. You have a story to tell, a product to sell, a service to provide, a difference to make and hearts and minds to influence. And there is no greater skill that you can learn to master that will help you influence humanity more than the power of effective public speaking and presentation.

In 2017 I was honored to serve as the Opening Keynote Speaker for the Toastmasters World Convention in British Columbia Vancouver, Canada. 2017 was exactly 20 years after I joined Toastmasters as a college student at Florida State University. Yep, I joined Toastmasters in 1997 in Tallahassee, Florida. Since that time, over the last 20 years, I've traveled the world as a full-time professional speaker and bestselling author. I've published over 7 books and sold tens of thousands of copies of those books. I've been blessed to appear on worldwide TV and I've also taught Public Speaking at the university level, produced TV infomercials and created and starred in the world's first Reality TV Show based on Public Speaking. It's called THE KEYNOTE and you can watch it right now at www.TheKeynoteTV.com.

I say all of this to stress that in 2017 I sat down and asked myself one powerful question. I said, "Del, out of the over 4,000 audiences you've spoken to all around the world, and the hundreds of students you've coached and professionally mentored, if you had to distill what you know about Public Speaking and Presentation Excellence into 52 Tips - 1 per week that *anybody* can learn and eventually master - what would those tips be? My greatest mentor of all time, Dr. Willie Jolley, taught me that tips stands for Techniques, Ideals, Principles and Strategies.

So in this book that you're about to enjoy - I've distilled my top 52 TIPS for not what to do, but rather WHO TO BE ... in order to develop what I like to call Platinum Presentations. Next level presentations that will fill your audience, calendar and bank account simultaneously. Regardless of your profession, your industry, your dreams or aspirations ... Public Speaking is indeed one of the most powerful and paramount SKILLS that you must develop. And please don't confuse the industry with the skill set. You don't have to want to be a motivational speaker as a *career* to develop your presentation skills.

So I invite you to dig into this book, and after each tip that you learn, I have provided space for you to journal about HOW you plan to implement what you've learned from that TIP into your next presentation. This book is very ACTIONABLE. Its instructionally designed so that you WIN and you get better with each page you read and apply.

When you enjoy what you learn from this book, I want to personally hear from you, so please go to www.PlatinumPresentationsBook.com and let me know what you think of this book. Also when you visit the website, we have cool bonuses, extra content and additional opportunities for you to take advantage of.

My friend, I'm excited for you and I hope that this book is the beginning of our journey and while I'm excited to see you apply all the amazing content in all your presentations - I'm equally excited to get the chance to work with you LIVE at my quarterly Presentation Skills Mastery event called *Crush The Stage.* Endorsed by Brian Tracy, Dr. Willie Jolley, Les Brown, The National Speakers Association and Toastmasters International - this 3-day deep dive is designed to exponentially accelerate your expert presentation skills and help you explode your income, impact and influence - regardless of your profession or industry.

Visit www.CrushTheStageLive.com right now to learn all about it and register for our limited-seating but unlimited-learning experience. Or call (813) 963-5356 for more details. In the meantime, let's get down to the business of changing your life and your presentation game forever.

Welcome again to Platinum Presentations and here's to your speaking ninjaness.

Delatorro

Forward by Les Brown:
Legendary Hall of Fame Motivational Speaker
Best Selling Author
TV Personality

I can recall meeting Delatorro back in 2000 in Tampa, Florida. He had just graduated Florida State University with honors and a Masters Degree in hand - he had a nice consulting position at a top company, but had a dream to be a speaker. He came to one of my speaking events and from there we went to lunch and then he registered to attend one of my Speaker Training Bootcamps. Over the course of those 3 days in my home in Maryland at that time, I realized that Delatorro had something very special and boy did I see greatness all over him.

Well, that was 18 years ago, and what Delatorro has done to not only grow himself, but also to impact the Speaking Industry as a whole is nothing short of amazing. You're holding in your hands book #7 that he has published. Over 4,000 paid presentations he has delivered all over the globe. Created and stars in the world's 1st Inspirational Business Reality TV Show based on Public Speaking called THE KEYNOTE. He's keynoted on the Main Platform of The Million Dollar Round Table and Toastmasters World Convention and the list goes on and on. But what I love most about that Delatorro is that he has not only succeed but he's helped so many aspiring Speakers, Authors, Coaches, Executives and Entrepreneurs to do the same.

Platinum Presentations represents 52 of Delatorro's Best TIPS and Tricks-of-the-Trade gleaned from over 20 years of platform experience. Yes, he started young, but he's paid the price to learn from the best and take what he learned and implement it at the highest level possible. You now, through this amazing new book, get the direct benefit of all that wisdom without having to go through the mistakes and pitfalls to get it.

There's another level for you and there is another level to your Presentation Skills. Regardless of your industry or profession, I am a living witness that the fastest and most powerful way to help humanity is to serve them and inspire them through the Power of your Public Speaking Skills. I am beyond certain that you will find this book to be powerful, actionable and transformational to the degree that you apply what it teaches you.

Congratulations, you're about to learn from one of the baddest speakers on the planet!

This is Ms. Mammie Brown's baby boy, there's greatness in you. Go get it and chase your dreams like they are the last bus of the night.

    -- Les Brown

Section 1:

Before Your Next Presentation

If you like this book,
you will LOVE the Audio Companion Coaching Program
Over 4 Hour of Transformative Coaching from Delatorro on 5 Audio CDs

Visit www.PlatinumPresentationsBook.com to Order Today.

1. BE CLEAR
About Your Purpose

My friend, clarity is power.

So let's start by getting crystal clear about the purpose of your presentation. What is your endgame?

You must be able to answer why you are giving this presentation to begin with. Are you seeking to educate, motivate, inspire, debate, debunk, provoke, arouse, support, rally, judge, criticize, sell, persuade, argue, antagonize, inform, showcase, recruit or the like?

All of these are valid motives for a presentation. So you must start by getting crystal clear about the **main** purpose of **your** presentation ... because without that your message has no end zone, home plate or basketball hoop. Dr. Steven Covey taught us to begin with the end in mind. This book is going to challenge you to do the same thing. Before you do anything else, get clear about WHY you are doing WHAT you are about to do in giving any presentation.

Start with a purpose statement like, "The goal of this presentation is to get WHO to do WHAT ... HOW?"

How Can I Be Clearer?

_____

_____

_____

_____

_____

_____

_____

_____

_____

_____

_____

_____

_____

_____

_____

_____

_____

_____

_____

_____

2. BE COMMITTED
To Giving Your Best

Every single presentation you give and every single audience you give it to, no matter how big or small … deserves for you to BRING IT!

So make the decision now that your presentation will be YOUR BEST!

James Brown was asked in an interview which concert was his BEST and he replied…the one I'll do tomorrow night. He always believed in topping himself.

Make the decision right now in this crafting stage of your presentation that this presentation will be BETTER than the last one you did in some way. Think about some small tweak you can make to your presentation to make it your BEST. Think about something your last audience taught you that you can apply to this next group. Think about something new you read, studied, watched or experienced that would be of benefit to this upcoming audience and gift them with your best.

How Can I Be More Committed?

_____

_____

_____

_____

_____

_____

_____

_____

_____

_____

_____

_____

_____

_____

_____

_____

_____

3. BE CURIOUS
About What The Audience Needs/Wants

Every single audience is different. I'm gonna say that again.

Every…single…audience…is…different.

I speak to corporations, associations, conventions, entrepreneur events and gatherings of all kinds. I also speak in churches. And when I speak at some churches, they have multiple services which means the guest speaker/minister (me in this case) has to be prepared to present the same message multiple times.

I remember a lovely church in South Florida where I had to deliver the same message to a Saturday night service and 3 Sunday morning services and I can tell you that although my message was the same, each audience was night-and-day different. Each audience had their own set of needs and desires from the service, from me and from God. It was my job to meet that audience where they were and to lift them to where I was inspired to lift them to. It was NOT my job to give the same cookie-cutter talk to each group. No matter how many times you have to present to a group, each new audience deserves something special (not a new presentation – that's craziness).

They deserve for you to play detective and to figure out what THEY need and want. To do that, sometimes conduct a survey, poll their Facebook group, send out a survey monkey email, do a conference call or webinar to the group in advance so you can ASK QUESTIONS! Be curious about WHY they are attending your event. What they need to get from your presentation. What they like about you and your presentation style. What mode they will most likely be in as they listen. What mistakes the last speaker made that you can avoid. Ways you can over-deliver for them. Be curious my friend.

How Can I Be More Curious?

4. BE OTHER FOCUSED
So You Can Customize Your Talk For Them

Ohhhhh, that dreaded word…Customization. Some speakers don't mind and others HATE to customize their talks. I actually LOVE the process of customizing my signature presentations to fit the needs of each new audience I am blessed to speak to.

The customization part is what allows me to be creative, like a chef. I get to go into the metaphorical kitchen and whip up a dish that isn't like the other 500 entrees I've made that day. This one is special. So look at it the same way when it's time to customize your presentation.

In fact, I want to challenge you to apply the Porato Principle to this tip. Use the 80/20 rule. Keep 80% of your presentation the same and customize 20% of it. Add the client's theme, some of their buzzwords or jargon, sprinkle in a few of their stories and big wins. Now in order to create this 20% magic, you've gotta care more about the client and the audience than how many stories you get to tell and how many slides you get to complete.

Remember, it's not about you. If you're too caught up in being The Speaker you won't customize because you will be pleased with your talk – as is. But when you are Other Focused, you build things into your program that are purely for the benefit of the audience. Never…ever give the exact same speech twice.

How Can I Be More Other Focused?

_____

_____

_____

_____

_____

_____

_____

_____

_____

_____

_____

_____

_____

_____

_____

_____

5. BE ORGANIZED
In How You Structure Your Presentation

Let me ask you one simple question. Do you want your audience to simply hear your presentation or do you want them to remember your presentation? The reason I ask this question is because I would venture to say that 90% of presentations I hear people give are not given for retention, they're given for reaction. Most speakers want the immediate reaction in the moment from the audience, but after that, they don't care too much about retention because if they did - their talk, presentation, speech, keynote or training would have been ORGANIZED in such a way that allowed for both reaction and more importantly retention of that information. Since we are building Platinum Presentations, let's build ones that are easy for the mind to retain. The simplest way to do that is to use The 3T Method.

Tell them what you're going to tell them – That's the **Intro**
Tell them – That's the **Body of your Presentation**
Tell them what you told them – That's the **Close**

It's really simple, yet some make it complex for no reason. Organize your content by deciding how many main points you want to share in your message and build your presentation by first alluding to the points in preview fashion - which is your opening. In the body of your talk, build a case for each point with stories, examples, stats, data and current events. In the conclusion, remind their brains of what you just put in them so that by the time you close, each brain has heard the points reiterated at least 3 times. Remember, repetition is the mother of skill and rehearsal is the father of learning.

How Can I Be More Organized?

_____

_____

_____

_____

_____

_____

_____

_____

_____

_____

_____

_____

_____

_____

_____

_____

_____

6. BE COLORFUL
In How You Decorate Your Presentation For POP

Okay, I want you to think of the main points of your presentation as the pants/skirt, shirt/blouse and shoes of your outfit. Now, I want you to think of everything else you put on your body when you really want to make a great impression. For ladies it could be things like your perfume, lipstick, makeup, watch, earrings, necklace, hairpins and other accessories. For guys it could be cologne, a watch, rings, bracelet, belt, sock game, pocket square or handkerchief. All of these things are ways that you accessorize your outfit.

Well, you can and should do the exact same thing to your presentations. Add POP, WOW and FLAIR to your talks and speeches by adding jokes, humor, powerful/punchy personal stories, props, illustrations, imagery and even sounds. All of these things allow you to accommodate various adult learning styles. Some people in your audience will resonate more with your quote when they hear you say it (auditory), some will resonate more when they see it on the screen (visual) and some will resonate more with it when they feel the Goosebumps on their arm as the power of that quote lands with them personally (kinesthetic).

Think of it like this: a house is simply a house, until you decorate it with your personal style. Once you do that, it becomes a home. So be colorful and vibrant with how you decorate your presentation so that you invite your entire audience in and they can feel relaxed and welcome.

How Can I Be More Colorful?

_____

_____

_____

_____

_____

_____

_____

_____

_____

_____

_____

_____

_____

_____

_____

_____

_____

7. BE THE EXPERT
Only Use Content That You've Mastered

Turn the gig down if you have to go bone up on the material. The reason is that we live in the Age of the Expert. The Era of the Result. People want you to get to the point and they want you to share what you know, not what you Googled. Anyone can Google anything these days. So pick an area of expertise and go deep into your understanding, study, research and comprehension of that content.

Remember, a jack of all trades is often a master of none. You can't be The Expert on everything. You have to decide what lane you want to ride in and pick an area of specialization based on your life story, your knowledge base and your personal and professional passions.

I love turning gigs down that are outside of my wheelhouse because it gives me a chance to refer another speaker friend, it allows me to be a resource for my client and it allows me to stay in my lane. When you are an expert on your subject matter, the hardest job you should have is not deciding what to put into your presentation, but what content to TAKE OUT to stay within the timeframe of your talk. That's when you know you are a master of your material. One final thought on being an expert in your subject … Don't be so much the expert that you come across arrogant or condescending. Be a humble expert that is passionate about people getting the info that you have to share, regardless of what the content is.

How Can I Be The Expert?

8. BE OPEN
To Exciting Ways To Teach An Old Concept …
In A New Way

While we are talking about content, I think it needs to be discussed that content for the most part is not what makes a great presentation. It's important, don't get me wrong, but once again, content is free on Google.

What makes a presentation is the openness of the presenter to present old information in a fun, engaging, interactive, spontaneous, memorable and magical way that inspires people to be better in some way.

Think about what makes a great sermon: it's not the scripture itself, because that's not new. Think about most sales or customer service or personal development content. The content itself is not rocket science my friend. It's not new, but it's you presenting it, teaching it, coaching it, training it and delivering it in a fresh and interesting way that makes for a rock star presentation that you can absolutely CRUSH.

When I speak for faculty retreats at universities and colleges one of the things I challenge faculty with is upgrading their pedagogy. The WAY they teach what they teach.

Think of some new ways to say the same old thing. Think about it, when a new restaurant hits your town you don't go there for steak, or chicken, or shrimp, or salmon or sushi. You go because of that particular restaurant's *spin* on those classic proteins.

How Can I Be More Open?

9. BE INQUISITIVE
Ask The Event Organizer Why You Were Picked

My friend, I need to give you a compliment. You are awesome. I mean that. There is something very unique and special about you. So much so, you were selected to give a presentation. Now that you have this opportunity, it's important that you bring YOU to the presentation. What do I mean by that?

What I mean is, in addition to the content and the flare, you must bring the cool, quirky, interesting, edgy and raw aspects of your own personality to the presentation as well. You see, the person that booked you for this opportunity chose you for a reason. You need to know what that reason is and build on that. If you've got great humor, wit and are pithy, then use that and build on that. If you've got awesome dry humor and candor, build on that. If you've got community aura about yourself that makes you memorable, bring that. If you have an energy that is infectious or a laugh that makes the audience laugh – use it. If you have a fashion-sense that makes people marvel at your attire as you present – leverage that. If you love flipcharts and markers – then ditch the PowerPoint slides and use what makes you – you.

Don't assume, make sure to ask why you were chosen. Ask why they picked you over someone else, and deliver on it. The reason they give you may not always be what you thought, but whatever they love about you and expect from you…DELIVER IT!

You won't know until you **ASK**.

    Actively **S**eek **K**nowledge.

How Can I Be More Inquisitive?

10. BE PASSIONATE
What Comes From The Heart, Reaches The Heart

My friend, everything is energy. Absolutely everything is energy! And if you present from a good energy place, it will land on your audience with good energy.

My brand is known for delivering high-content presentations with incredible amounts of raw, sincere and intentional heart-centered energy and passion. I don't need coffee to produce it, I don't need exercise to produce it and I don't need the perfect audience to produce it either. It's just there. And I want to encourage you to tap into your own personal high-energy place and bring that to your presentations. Nobody wants good information that is boring to hear. Now, I'm not saying that you have to bounce off the walls or take a bottle of 5-hour Energy before you hit the stage, but rather bring energy for what good energy means to you. It will show up in your smile, your tone of voice, your stance, your stride, your demeanor and other non-verbal ways.

If the content that you are talking about doesn't move you, it won't move your audience. So only present material that you've mastered like I already mentioned, but also whatever you share, please do it with a cheerful, grateful and energetic heart of service to humanity and you will rock the room. *Remember: what comes from the heart, reaches the heart.*

Which reminds me of something else. Before you wow people with your intellect, capture their hearts first. Once you have their heart, you can teach them anything. Each one, reach one. Once you reach them with your heart-centered spirit, you can mold, shape and transform their minds at will.

How Can I Be More Passionate?

11. BE PREPARED
By Practicing With Loosely Scripted Notes

Practice does not make you perfect, but practice certainly does make you better. Much *much* better. Listen friend, this presentation counts. So prepare for it like you would anything else important in your life. What will allow you to stand strong and confident in your presentation delivery is how much preparation and practice you put in before the actual presentation. Regardless of whether your presentation is 10 minutes or a full day. Regardless of if it's a conference call, webinar, live presentation or media interview - you want to make sure that you KNOW your content. Focus 80% of your attention on the audience and only 20% on your notes. For example: if you're spending 40% of your eye contact looking at your PowerPoint slides, looking down at the podium or scrolling through your iPad notes or whatever - you have not memorized enough of your material and you are too notes dependant. Are you? Are you too notes dependant? If so, I want you to break yourself FREE by doing the following. I want you to practice and present with what I call Loosely Scripted Notes.

Your notes should be used to trigger thoughts. It's that simple. I don't write out my speeches. I have not written out a speech word-for-word in over 20 years.

I write power phrases that trigger thoughts and bursts of well-known content. Rather than typing out a full story, I just type out: Winn-Dixie Story – Multiple Income Streams. From seeing that one line I can speak for 5 minutes by telling the story, adding audience interaction and teaching the business lesson. Here's another example, I can write down: 5 Ways to Get Anything You Want and from that one power phrase, I can speak for 10 minutes. Taking about 2 minutes to teach each of the 5 principles. See my point? You don't have to write down word-for-word what you are going to say, just write down phrases that trigger dialogue. **On the next page –**I want you to practice creating loosely scripted notes and jumping off from them. Oh, and remember: use BIG FONT. You'd be surprised how bad your vision gets once you get in front of an audience.

How Can I Be Better Prepared?

_____

_____

_____

_____

_____

_____

_____

_____

_____

_____

_____

_____

_____

_____

_____

_____

_____

12. BE AVAILABLE
To Consult With Your Client Beforehand
To Help Them Succeed

One of the things that will get you invited back, rebooked and requested to present again is not only how good your live presentation is, but also (and people often drastically underestimate this) how EASY you are to work with leading up to the event. Remember, unless the person booking you is a paid professional meeting planner, the person that is coordinating your slot at an event is volunteering their time and energy to make the event happen. They are planning your speaking appearance in addition to doing their regular job and managing their personal life. How easy you are to work with is a key factor in getting you rebooked and your calendar filled faster.

Remember ⟹ Rebookings = Revenue.

The days, weeks and months leading up to your presentation, make sure that you are available to help participate in conference calls or Skype meetings with your client to consult and be a thought-partner to make the event a big success. Share marketing ideas, advertising strategies, internet marketing tricks, social media strategies, video marketing ideas and the like to help them make the event as awesome as possible. In truth, that only helps YOU! I remember I gave one client one idea that saved their convention budget more money than my speaking fee. They were so grateful that they rebooked for the following year BEFORE I even spoke, and I got other referrals from them.

To this day, I have clients that rebook me because after booking other speakers that turned out to be prima donnas – they missed how accessible and down-to-earth I was to work with: Rebookings = Revenue.

How Can I Be More Available?

_____

_____

_____

_____

_____

_____

_____

_____

_____

_____

_____

_____

_____

_____

_____

_____

_____

13. BE BIG PICTURE
Think About How Your Presentation Fits
Into The Entire Event

Okay - so this next tip is the massive secret sauce to my success as a speaker and I'm sharing it with you… As you prepare for your next presentation, regardless of what it is, think about and build into your presentation what I call a Big Picture Perspective. *What is that?* It's when you take into account all the various other aspects of your event and you somehow BUILD other elements of the event into your presentation. Meaning … maybe you listen to the person that speaks before you and you incorporate something they said into your message. Maybe you comment on some big achievement posted on the website of the organization you are speaking to as a way of celebrating them. Maybe you take a quick 20-second video of you using the product or service that your client sells to show how cool you think it is. These are all easy, simple, yet Powerful ways that you can bring a Big Picture perspective to your presentation.

Additionally consider how your presentation fits into all the other elements of the event, conference, convention, service, program or session. Do you know what happens right before and right after you speak? Do you know the mood of the audience? Are you speaking right before or right after lunch, dinner or an important break? How will that affect the motivation of the audience. These are all things to consider. Has the audience been beat up all day with content? If so, you may need to be more entertaining and less educational because their brains are already fried. We will talk more about this in the next section when we talk about rhetorical sensitivity. Your presentation is not an isolated experience. It's a part of a bigger picture.

Understand that bigger picture and build that into your message and get ready to **CRUSH THE STAGE!**

How Can I Be More Big Picture?

14. BE SIMPLE
Breakdown Complex Principles, Concepts and Ideologies

I know that I've spent a great deal of time encouraging you to be the expert and that's crucial, but now I want to encourage you to comb through your presentation and take everything that's deep, complex, complicated, PhD-level and advanced ... and find some cool, pop-culture, 21st century ways to make your high-level content palatable to your audience. A key to being a great speaker is to take complex principles and simplify them so that everyone gets it. Everyone should relate to and properly digest your content. There is nothing wrong with being an academic. However, if you want to be a transformational communicator – take your deep stuff and hold your audience's hand and usher them gradually into your deeper more profound world of ninjaness. Keep in mind, you've been studying your material for years, this may be some people's first exposure to your concepts. So break it down. Use metaphors, analogies, examples and for-instance statements to explain the same concept at least 3 different ways. *Why?*

Because your audience needs to hear it more than one way. The more examples you can provide, the deeper the content will sink. As you are building your presentation, give yourself time to Unpack the Suitcase. What I mean by that is: every suitcase lies by making you think that what's inside is the same size as the suitcase. That's not true. There is always way more stuff in a suitcase than it shows when it's closed. There is so much more to your concept than how it first looks when presented. Take time and build time into your presentation to unpack your suitcase. If you say something deep…KNOW that you did, and take the time to unpack what that means.

Nothing spells amateur more than someone who doesn't know that they've said something powerful and you leave your audience confused and leaning over to each other trying to figure out what's happened. Be simple. The more simple you are the easier it is for your audience to apply what you've taught them.

How Can I Be Simpler?

15. BE ORIGINAL
There Are Enough Wannabes Out There

This one is huge. Well they are all huge, but pay attention. I want you to really think about where you get your content. I think content is king and I want you to be a high-content presenter. In order to do that, you need to reverse the typical process we go through to acquire content for our presentations. I would venture to bet that most of us read books, articles, newspapers and watch videos or listen to the gurus of our time, then distill what we've heard and produce our presentations based on what they say and then we salt and pepper their content with OUR stories and call it an original presentation. Well friends, that's not an original presentation. That's a knockoff.

A better idea. A much better idea:

Take a blank sheet of paper; make a list from 1 to 10 and ask yourself this one question. "How did I do that?" Why? Because much of what you will teach an audience is based on what you accomplished or achieved right? You've done something right like lost weight, built a successful business, hit an income goal, raised a successful family, published something, hit a major milestone in your company or crushed another goal. You did something that you want to teach others how to do. So make a list of HOW you did WHAT you did.

Once you have your list of steps, strategies or principles that you know and have applied, *then* you go to the books and internet as support for your formula versus using their formula and adding your stories to it. If you use your formula, plus your stories, you will only need about 10% guru/Google support for your content to make it awesome. Be original. The world already knows what the greats believe; your audience wants to know what *you* believe. You got this gig because people want to hear from you. So be you and bring YOUR content to the presentation and it will go very very well.

How Can I Be More Original?

_____

_____

_____

_____

_____

_____

_____

_____

_____

_____

_____

_____

_____

_____

_____

_____

16. BE GRATEFUL
For The Opportunity To Impact People As A Leader

The greatest human emotion that you can build and prepare a presentation from is the emotion of gratitude. Plain and simple, gratitude should be the primary emotion from which you pull inspiration as you seek to impact lives with your presentations. Regardless of the topic, your ability to infuse celebratory, appreciative and uplifting sentiments into your content is paramount to your next talk. Remember this my friend, public speaking is still the #1 fear in America, Canada and other parts of the world. To be chosen as the person to hold the microphone and impact and lead humanity towards greater success in any area or aspect of life is a blessing indeed. So here are a few things you can add into your presentation that will build gratitude into your talk.

Start your presentation with a thank you to the audience for what you know is about to happen - for them investing their time into the opportunity to learn and hear from you. That gratitude will have them paying more attention and listening better. Also, express gratitude for all the lessons that you've learned that you will be sharing. If you are bitter about the road you took to learn the lessons that you did, it will show in your tonality. Rather, reframe all the negative energy you have around your process and understand that none of us get a free lunch in life. We all have to go through the school of hard knocks to learn the best lessons. Reframe your process and look at it as a challenge that built character. No matter what it was, tell your audience that you are thankful for the dark times in your life because we can't appreciate the day without understanding the night. We can't appreciate sunshine unless we've survived the storms. Winter makes us appreciate spring and fall. Get my point?

Build more gratitude into your presentation and it will make you smile more - smiling is a universal language.

How Can I Be More Grateful?

_____

_____

_____

_____

_____

_____

_____

_____

_____

_____

_____

_____

_____

_____

_____

_____

17. BE EARLY
So You Have Time To Set Up Your Environment For Success

One of the smartest and best habits to develop as a speaker, communicator, teacher, lecturer, presenter, trainer, expert, consultant, marketer, educator, designer, builder and/or transformer is the habit of arriving to your presentations EARLY. It's true that the early bird gets the worm, but also the early bird gets first crack at setting up the environment for success. If you arrive just before your presentation time, you've had no time to cultivate the environment. Arrive early and do a few of these things to make your next presentation awesome.

1. Connect with the AV team and make sure you conduct your own sound check of all the AV equipment to make sure that it's working at an optimum level.

2. Feel the room. Walk around the entire area and feel the room. What color are the walls, what aroma does the space have, what energy is it giving off? Does that energy support or distract from your message?

3. Coordinate with the person that booked you to learn about last minute changes, twists, turns, mishaps or such that will impact your presentation. Double check the amount of time you actually have because sometimes what you were promised during planning changes once you are live.

4. Set up your Information/Resources/Product Table in an HTA **(High Traffic Area)** so that once you are done and even before you present, you can be conducting business, exchanging business cards, generating leads, selling and promoting.

5. Another massive reason you want to arrive early is so important that I gave it its own page...

How Can I Be Earlier?

_____

_____

_____

_____

_____

_____

_____

_____

_____

_____

_____

_____

_____

_____

_____

_____

_____

18. BE SOCIAL
Walk Around And Meet The People You're About To Speak To

Save the greenrooms and private holding suites for everyone else. For *you*, I want you *Out* and *About* - mingling and meeting the people you are about to present to. Getting to know their stories. Learn more about why they are attending the event and what they hope to gain.

The thing I love about meeting my audience before the presentation is that it allows me to *turn a cold audience into a warm audience*. It allows me to get out of my own head and get into the hearts and minds of those I am there to SERVE! Remember, the more you approach this opportunity as a chance to serve versus a chance to speak you will be less nervous and anxious and you will be more on fire to help, transform and ultimately persuade. It's going to feel awkward in the beginning because the audience won't be used to you walking up to them in mid-conversation with their colleagues but trust me, they will love that you took the first step to break the ice and in spite of your impressive bio and credentials wanted to approach them. Also, this is a huge moneymaker - I have noticed that the more people I shake hands with BEFORE my speech, the more people show up at my table AFTER my speech.

Inevitability, what you will notice is that the people that you shake hands with before your presentation are also the same people that will be your biggest note takers, supporters, listeners and cheering section DURING your presentation as well, because they feel like they know you. Save the greenroom for the superstars, if you want Platinum Presentations where audiences clap with their hands, hearts and ultimately their wallets – get out and meet your tribe before you get introduced.

How Can I Be More Social?

19. BE READY
What Happens When They Like You?

If you do half of what I already taught you in the first section of this amazing book, your audience is going to love you. Here's my next question. Have you put enough time and energy into preparing for what will happen when your audience likes you? Are you ready to be loved by a crowd of 10 to 10,000 at the same time? No matter how many people you are speaking to, your audience will always, and I do mean always, outnumber you. Sooooo, what happens when they like you? Have you prepared for it?

Go into this presentation visualizing that it will go extremely well. Go into this presentation expecting people to come up to you afterwards wanting your time and attention. Go into this presentation expecting people to visit your resource table and investing in themselves. Go into this presentation expecting to take a lot of photos afterwards. It's gonna happen. So again, now what? What's next for them…the audience?

What should they do AFTER you have wowed them? If you don't have a clear-cut plan for exactly what happens next then you need to consider enrolling in my business development coaching experience called *Speaking Business Mastery*. In it, I teach you exactly how to build an empire for your audiences to fall into once they have been blown away and impressed by you. Once they have some of you, they will want MORE of you.

Let's work together so I can help you build the backend business that you will need to support your audience because being outnumbered is a good problem to have, that means people need your products and services.

How Can I Be Ready?

Visit PlatinumPresentationsBook.com to get additional resources Delatorro has created to help you maximize this content and take your presentations to the Platinum level.

Section 2:

During Your

Next Presentation

If you like this book,
you will LOVE the Audio Companion Coaching Program
Over 4 Hour of Transformative Coaching from Delatorro on 5 Audio CDs

Visit www.PlatinumPresentationsBook.com to Order Today.

20. BE INTRODUCED
Write Your Own Intro That Sets The Tone And Sells You

Your introduction is how your audience first learns more about you. Well, now-a-days that's not exactly true. The real truth is that many audience members will have already Googled you, vetted and researched you long before they sit in front of you. What I'm finding is that many people in the typical audience are not learning of you for the first time in your introduction. However, your written introduction is still very very important and it sets the tone for your presentation. If done correctly it can also sell your products, services and future bookings as well. It all depends on how well it's written and read.

Make sure that you take the time to *write your own introduction* and travel with it, keep it on you to email, text or hand deliver to your introducer. It should be about 5 - 7 sentences and should offer information about you biographically, yet also explain the value of the presentation they are about to hear. It should frame the mind of your audience showing them you have the credibility and experience to be the speaker for this event. Make sure that you go over the intro with your introducer because if they do a great job, your audience will be primed and ready to receive what you have to share. If they do a poor job, your audience could be confused, annoyed and unsure of who you are and why they should pay attention. If you've been speaking for a while, you may want to consider doing a video introduction. That way, people won't mispronounce your name, give you doctorate degrees that you don't have or tell the audience "the speaker wanted me to read this about them," all of which I have had happen to me.

Regardless of whether it's a written intro or video, make sure it's presented and delivered well because again, it sets the best tone for your overall presentation.

How Can I Be Introduced Properly?

_____

_____

_____

_____

_____

_____

_____

_____

_____

_____

_____

_____

_____

_____

_____

21. BE CONFIDENT
Remember You're Not Nervous You Simply Have An H.A.O.I.O.

Your audience only knows what you tell them. Right? Well that's partly true. The full truth is that yes, your audience only knows what you disclose, so if you don't disclose what's wrong, most times they won't know exactly. For example, your audience will only know that you have a headache if you tell them. They will only know that your shirt is wrinkled in the back if you tell them. They will only know that you are arguing with your spouse if you tell them. Don't over advertise what's going on with you personally to your audience.

However, as a caveat, please also keep in mind that audiences can sense non-verbal body language – it shows when you are nervous, anxious and/or scared. It will show up in your stance, your tone, your timbre, your facial expressions and your overall body language. Your non-verbal action could totally distract them from what you are saying verbally. Rather than displaying being nervous, BE CONFIDENT!

Stand, walk, talk and gesture with total and absolute confidence. Why? Because the truth is you're not nervous, you simply have … remember this tip's title? You have a **Healthy Anticipation of an Incredible Outcome.**

In other words, you have a blissful exuberance about things going well. So be confident. Even while you're sitting in your seat before you speak, sit with confidence. Network before your presentation with confidence and assuredness. That confidence will come through in everything you do and say during your presentation and *that* will win over your audience.

How Can I Be More Confident?

_____

_____

_____

_____

_____

_____

_____

_____

_____

_____

_____

_____

_____

_____

_____

_____

22. BE COGNIZANT
Of The Climate And Culture Of The Room And Shift It To Your Will

Decide right now. Will you shift your energy to where the audience is, or will you require the energy of the audience to shift up to where you are? I think you know by now which I am recommending.

The reality is that you have prepared more for your audience than your audience has prepared for you. Most times you will have more passion, energy and enthusiasm for what you will be sharing than your audience.

Therefore, it's your job to shift your audience UP to your level. It may take a few minutes for them to catch your style, flair and persona —don't give up. If you're a speaker that likes audience interaction, stick with it throughout your presentation and about 10 to 15 minutes in, they will catch on. If you like to walk all over the room and you're concerned that the first few rows can't see you, just keep walking and if you are compelling enough, they will turn their bodies and chairs to face you and take notes in their lap if they have to.

Recently at a leadership conference the speaker before me was really low energy. The audience response was really poor, people didn't seem interested and this was the kickoff for the event. Once I saw that, and I felt the climate of the room, I made a commitment to not allow the climate to change me. I got on stage and did my thing and they loved it. It took the audience about 7 minutes of my 90-minute presentation to reach full buy-in and catch on to my interactive style, but once they did … wow, it was an incredible experience.

Be cognizant … ultimately make it your business to shift the atmosphere of your audience to match your level of passion, enthusiasm and energy.

How Can I Be More Cognizant?

23. BE EXPRESSIVE
By Utilizing Your Entire Body
In Your Presentation

Always remember this, your body is your best visual aid. It just is. So use your entire body in your presentation. Your face, your hands and arms. Your walk, your stance, your feet are all working together to help you succeed in your presentation. Additionally, keep in mind that your expressions should adjust to the size audience you are speaking to. You don't need 10,000 gestures and body positions for 100 people. You will overpower your audience and make them run away. *Lol.* But at the same time you don't want to give 10,000 people the same energy you would reserve for 100 people because they will quickly tune you out.

If you want your audience to raise their hands enthusiastically, you do it first. If you want your audience to say YES with energy and excitement, you say it that way first. If you want your audience to go around and hug or high-five people, you go around and do it first.

You must lead by example and show your audience what good expression looks like. For example, I love to smile a lot in my speeches. I've noticed that the more I smile, the more my audience feels like they have permission to smile back. Another thing that happens to me is that I sweat during my presentations. Not because I'm nervous, but rather because I am so passionate about what I am talking about. I tell my audience to expect that as a part of my expression. I know speakers who take their shoes off on stage as a part of their expression. I know speakers that sing at the end of their presentation to express a different side of their talents and gifts to their audience. Whatever allows you to express yourself in the best way…do that.

How Can I Be More Expressive?

24. BE INCLUSIVE
Of The Entire Room The Entire Time
Front To Back And Side To Side

We've already established that you will always be outnumbered by your audiences. However, an expert communicator like yourself will never allow the audience to feel like they are outnumbering you or overwhelming you. In order to do that, you must include your entire audience into your presentation. If you want revenue from the entire room, you need to engage the entire room. If you want leads, business cards, contact information and applause from the entire room you must deliver to the entire room – front to back and side to side.

Many speakers focus on the first few rows and everyone else basically watches the speaker give a talk to their front-row friends. That's whack.

Instead, I want you to communicate to the entire room. Sometimes that may mean asking those in the middle and the back to raise their hands or shout back at you. It may mean walking around and using the entire stage that you are given. It may mean projecting your voice more. It may mean increasing the font size of your presentation slides to make sure the person in the last row can see the content. It may mean … watch this … staying ON the stage because the cameras and IMAG can follow you and keep you lit better if you stay on stage versus getting down and walking around.

No matter what your audience size, include the entire room and the entire room will want to do business with you later.

How Can I Be More Inclusive?

25. BE IN CHARGE
Don't Let The Audience Take You To A Place That Your Client Will Regret

You were brought in for a reason. Always remember in every presentation you have two audiences. You have the event host/meeting planner who booked you (your client) and you also have the audience of people that are listening to your presentation. Sometimes the person that books you doesn't even get a chance to hear all of your presentation because they are running around doing other things for the event. However, pleasing that person is very important because they are the ones that hired/scheduled you and it's their objectives that you want to make sure you deliver on. Additionally, you want to please the audience in front of you and rock the presentation for them too, because it's often the evaluations from that group which will determine if the meeting planner/event host will rebook you.

I've seen speakers get in front of an audience and start feeling the crowd and play so much to the crowd that they completely forget to finish delivering the content that they promised the event host.

Don't get so caught up in getting a reaction from the audience that you miss the goal and the aim of the meeting planner and mess up your chances of returning.

Playing to both audiences is not hard once you are aware that you have two *and both matter.* Stay in charge of your presentation and don't let the hype of the crowd derail your overall agenda.

How Can I Be More In Charge?

26. BE PROMPT
Because Everyone's Time Is Valuable

It's easy to get so caught up in your stories, metaphors, examples, humor, audience participation and content that you completely forget about or underestimate the time. It's very easy to go OVER on your time. However, the challenges with going over on your time are several fold.

➢ If you go over by as little as 15 minutes you could easily lose the only break between you and the next speaker. That break was also your sales/marketing break. So by going over on stage, you kill your own sales at the back of the room. Less time to sell, lead-generate, network and create spinoff opportunities.

➢ Another reason you don't want to go over is because if another speaker is using the same room you are – you have just cut into their time to set up for their presentation. That prevents the next speaker from having a good and punctual start to their presentation.

➢ Another reason to stay on time is because going over could throw off other important happenings like lunch, an awards ceremony or media interviews. All of these things run on tight schedules, so keeping in time allows all the other aspects of the event to run smoothly.

Remember it's better to end early than finish late. Everyone's time is valuable – respect theirs as well as yours.

How Can I Be Prompt?

27. BE CANDID
Fluff Doesn't Create Change – Real Talk Does
Don't Be Afraid To Be Gritty

Fluff doesn't create change – don't be afraid to be gritty. Now is the best time for you to be real, honest and raw with your audience. It doesn't matter if your subject matter is parenting, financial services, real estate, insurance, spiritual growth, work/life balance, fitness, nutrition, marriage, singleness, line-dancing, politics, social media, internet marketing, leadership, sales, customer service, criminal justice or fill-in-the-blank.

Each of these topic areas and millions more allow for a real and candid approach that will cut through rhetoric and dogma and get to the heart of the matter. Like I told you in the first section, we now live in the Age of Expert and the Era of Results. Because of this, people pay attention to people that know what they are talking about and whose information produces an outcome that they want. Ted Talks and social media have forever changed the game because any speeches can be condensed to the best 17 minutes of it and social media says that if it's important you can say it in 144 characters or in a 1-minute video.

People's attention spans have been drastically reduced. This reduction lends itself to audiences appreciating people getting to the point much faster. Direct is best. Let me ask you a question. If you turned on your GPS and put in a destination and you had two options, a longer, fluff-filled route or a shorter-faster route – which would you pick? Of course you would pick the shorter route. Additionally, even when you are en route somewhere, if you see that you can "Save 9 minutes by re-routing" don't you take that option? I know I do…all the time. We like to be direct. We like to get from where we are directly to where we want to end up. Do you prefer flights with connections or non-stops? Non-stops right? Me too. We are so much alike. But honestly, think about it. You like these options because they get rid of anything that's not necessary and go right to the point. That's what your presentation must do. So be candid. Tell it like it is – people appreciate less polish and more grit these days.

How Can I Be More Candid?

28. BE PUNCHY
Audiences Like To Remember Phrases, Tweetables, One-Liners And Power Thoughts

When I first started speaking, what I studied more than anything was quote books. I remember my mom used to buy me quote books from different bookstores because she knew that I loved powerful quotes. What I loved most about them was that a quote can say so much in just one sentence or two at the most. Back in high school I would read a powerful quote and then I would practice expounding on that quote for a minute or two to see what I could say about that quote if ever asked to speak on it.

That one exercise helped me to develop what's called extemporaneous or impromptu speaking skills. So for over 20 years I've been known for my catch phrases, one-liners and punchy powerful statements. Social media didn't exist back when I developed this gift, now it lends itself perfectly to social media because audiences all over the world will tweet out and share and even create photo quotes during my presentation of powerful punchy statements that they will always remember.

Being Punchy is Being Candid's cousin, because the more to-the-point you can be in your live delivery, the more punchy your content will be also.

Being Punchy has many benefits. People will share your content more, they will take more notes, they will retain it better and the news media is 10x more likely to quote you from short, powerful and punchy statements that get to the heart and soul of your message.

How Can I Be Punchier?

29. BE PROFOUND
Information Is Free
People Can Google Content – What They Need Is Your Profound Wisdom Gleaned From Experience

Share information gleaned from experience. We've covered being candid and being punchy, you also must be Profound. Yes…I want you to be deep, powerful, transformative. I've told you several times in this book that information itself is free - abundant online. Audiences don't just need more information. They need wisdom.

Wisdom is knowledge correctly applied to a situation that produces a desired outcome. Wisdom can also be knowledge incorrectly applied to a situation with a life-lesson learned as a result. This stuff is harder to Google. Your audience wants the end outcome, not your process of trial and error. In fact, they want you to save them the headaches and the heartaches and give them the shortcut. That's why articles, posts and Pinterests that are successful are the ones with lists. Profound content is the unexpected twist on old or popular concepts that the audience is not expecting. Profound content is taking a unique vantage point that you have not seen or heard before. Profound content is disagreeing with globally accepted belief and having the audacity to think a new way and stand out there by yourself to defend it until it becomes widely accepted. Profound content is spotting trends, patterns and cycles of the human experience that stand out and are noteworthy. Profound content is explaining something complex in a very simple way. As you are delivering *DARE to be DEEP*.

Make your audience go home and look up terms, definitions, phenomenon and happenings. Make them hungry to be learned and well-studied like you. When you're sharing profound content – you know it. How? You get chills and this wave of transformation comes over you - you know in that very moment that people's lives will never be the same, because as Oliver Wendell Homes said, *"As soon as the mind is exposed to a new idea, it can't shrink back to its original state!"*

How Can I Be More Profound?

_____

_____

_____

_____

_____

_____

_____

_____

_____

_____

_____

_____

_____

_____

_____

_____

30. BE WELL-READ
Audiences Love To Learn The
Sources Of Your Content

Audiences already respect you because you're doing something that would make most of them cringe and they love to learn. However, your respect level will grow when your audience realizes that you are a rich treasure chest of supplemental information – other than your own. People love to know sources. How you got that smart. How you came to know what you know. How you developed your philosophy on business or life or faith or finances or fill-in-the-blank. They want to know where you feed, because if they can learn where you feed and begin to feed there too, they can one day be as intelligent/achieved/wealthy/connected as you are.

Since that's what they want, give it to them. Let's lead them to the well where they can drink and drink until their hearts and minds are full. At least 3 or 4 times during your presentation use a phrase like, "I remember reading in (Author's Name) book called (Name of Book), this powerful principle that changed my life and business. It talks about (quick summary of that point). When you get a chance you should read that book, it can change your life, like it has mine."

You will be amazed at how many people will write down the name of the author and the book. What percentage of those people actually buy it is a much different conversation, but in that moment, your stock just went up 1,000 points because you recommended something to them that will benefit their life, that you have ZERO financial benefit from or connection to in most cases. It's just a gift. And the more you share stuff like this – the more your titles go away and are replaced with designations like trusted advisor, mentor, sage and/or guru. In that moment, you're not a sales professional, speaker, author, expert, coach or consultant – you're a trusted resource for information. Leverage that positioning in their minds because it will pay off later.

How Can I Be More Well-Read?

31. BE DETERMINED
To Leave That Audience Better Than The Way
You Found It

Leave the audience better than how you found it. I am a lion with my audiences. I am a hungry beast that is determined to EAT. Do you know what feeds me as a speaker? Seeing (in real time) my audiences GET IT!

➢ Seeing the light bulbs go off.
➢ Seeing people's individual *ah hahs*.
➢ Watching people's physiology shift towards me.
➢ Witnessing people's mindset change right in front of me.
➢ Noticing how they realize their old patterns can be broken.
➢ Seeing someone realize that they are not alone in their experience.
➢ Seeing the walls of race, culture, gender give way to equality.
➢ Seeing people feel the connection of the human experience.

All of this comes when you are determined to leave your audience better than the way you found them. And when you are determined you add things to your presentation that you didn't rehearse, practice, plan or prepare for. Because regardless of how much you practice, NOTHING can 100% prepare you for THE MOMENT. Accept the moment. I want you to be determined. Be like a magician that has tons of tricks up their sleeve to offer and dazzle their audience. Be willing to tell a story you didn't plan for. You learned during networking that 30% of your audience will be able to relate to that. I can't tell you how many times I've added metaphors, examples, stories and content that was not originally planned, just because I knew it would help *that* audience GET IT. The more they GET IT, the more they will WANT YOU.

The more they want you, the more they will want what you offer! It's that simple.

How Can I Be More Determined?

32. BE ACTIONABLE
People Want Content That They
Can Implement Immediately

People want content they can implement immediately. My friend, the days of being articulate and that being enough to fill your audience are OVER! Now-a-days you can't just be a slick-tongued, witty, pithy orator and expect people to be transformed, changed or inspired to want to do business with you. You must be actionable. You must be outcome/end-goal focused. Now more than ever, people want results-based information, so don't just teach principles, also back out of those principles and give people actionable ideas that they can use immediately. Give people:

5 steps	2 realities
4 keys	7 ideas
3 strategies	4 models
8 mistakes	9 mysteries
6 secrets	

Make your audience write lists. The reason you want them to list things is because the more they list things, the more VALUE they feel they got. Additionally, the more lists you give them, the more their mind will attack it because as human beings, we love lists. The best infographics, Pinterests and articles come in list form.

The final reason you want to give your audience a list of things is because of what I like to call the overwhelm effect. Once they take too many notes, they will start to feel overwhelmed. As long as your products and services offer solutions in list form, you will make a lot of money by having them invest in your Done For You solutions. Lastly, you want people taking action on your material because ACTION leads to results, results lead to testimonials and endorsements, and those lead to repeat referrals and spin-off business. Don't just be philosophical – be actionable. Action creates reaction and reaction creates rebookings and revenue!

How Can I Be More Actionable?

_____

_____

_____

_____

_____

_____

_____

_____

_____

_____

_____

_____

_____

_____

_____

_____

33. BE AUTHENTIC
Because People Can Smell A Fake And A Phony
A Mile Away

People can smell a fake a mile away. My mother, Olivia B. McNeal, transitioned to heaven in April of 2013. Years leading up to her passing, I was filled with emotion for the pain she was in as her body begin to breakdown organ-by-organ. I remember many presentations where I would shed several tears as I talked about her to my audiences. That raw, real and authentic emotion won over so many of my audiences and it gave them permission to be real and authentic too.

After she passed, something interesting happened. I found myself telling a story about her and expecting myself to tear up like I normally would, however, the tears didn't come. Gig after gig I would talk about Thriving Through Your Storms (the part where I normally talk about my mom) and inside myself, I would wonder why I wasn't crying anymore. Has this ever happened to you regarding sharing something emotional?

What I realized is that I was healing more and more with each day and it didn't hurt as much as it did before she passed and shortly afterwards. I was faced with an ethical and authentic situation. Do I fake the old emotions to get the audience to do what they used to, or do I become authentic and find other ways to connect with my audiences? The choice was easy. Be real. Be authentic. I embraced the fact that I had healed from her passing and shifted that expectation from the audience. Months later, I was talking about her and expected not to cry and something happened and I broke in front of an audience that I was sure I would hold it together for. What's the point, you ask?

Be real.   Be authentic.   Be sincere.

When something hurts, tell your audience that. When you've healed from it, tell your audience that. When you're in between, share that stage too. You're a communicator but you're still a human being.

How Can I Be More Authentic?

34. BE HUMBLE
Enough To Take Yourself Off The Pedestal
Others Place You On

Take yourself off the pedestal others place you on. There are many very cool, exciting, energizing and ego-boosting things that happen when you are asked to speak for an organization. Think about it, they normally ask for your photo so they can print it in the program, you are normally featured on flyers, social media graphics and sometimes they even put you in the paper or create press releases with your photo, bio and websites. You can even be asked to participate in local, national and even international news media to help promote the event. All of this stuff is really awesome and it feels good. Years after, it's still cool to see it ... HOWEVER ...

I want to challenge and encourage you to stay HUMBLE. You can easily allow all this event worship to get to your head and heart and it will begin to change you. I've seen it happen. Power comes along with speaking. Money comes along with speaking. Attraction comes along with speaking. Notoriety comes along with speaking. And so does a very faulty, temporary and one-sided perspective as to who you really are. That audience is not in love with you. They don't know the *real,* full you. They know the BRAND that was promoted. So don't believe all the hype and don't allow all the fanfare to get to your head. It can destroy you. Don't make a permanent change in your personality based on a fleeting and temporary affect from the audience. Don't fall in love with the praise, fall in love with the impact you make on them. Don't fall in love with the applause, fall in love with the transformation you can make on your audience.

I've seen so many speakers rise and crash fast, not because they were bad speakers, they were actually very good. But they had attitudes, dispositions, egos and reputations that turned audiences, clients and business the other way. Never believe your own hype, press and promotion.

How Can I Be Humbler?

_____

_____

_____

_____

_____

_____

_____

_____

_____

_____

_____

_____

_____

_____

_____

_____

_____

_____

35. BE RELATABLE
Remember A Talk Lasts An Hour But An Experience Lasts A Lifetime

A huge benefit of applying the last principle I taught you in your next presentation is that it leads naturally and effortlessly to this principle. One of the key reasons you are giving your presentation is to do *what?* Hopefully, the goal is for people to learn more about who you are and what you do and offer and want to do business with you in some form or fashion after you are done speaking. Right?

Well, people do business with folks they know, like and trust. The stories you tell, the examples you give and the window into yourself that you share allows the people in your audience to transition from learning from you, to getting to know you, to getting to like you and then to trust you, count on you and rely on your perspective. Hopefully, by the time you finish, your audience will see you as a trusted advisor. Someone who they can depend on for wisdom, insight, confidence, direction and leadership. Sometimes the best way to be more relatable is to find the thing that people admire most about you – and tell stories that shed light on your process. Most audiences marvel over your end product. Who you became, what you achieved and all the accolades you've collected. That's what makes them "worship" you. However, what makes you relatable is the JOURNEY. The process of getting to where you are is what inspires people to understand that "she's just like me" or "he's got the same hangups I do." "And with those hangups, setbacks, challenges and obstacles, if they can do it – then so can I." That's the POWER of being relatable. So if you're wealthy, share stories of being broke and getting to wealth. If you're happily married, share stories of when you were single and some of the hurdles you overcame to have an amazing marriage. If you have super confidence, share stories and examples of when you didn't believe in yourself and when you struggled with your own self-esteem. Trust me my friend, if you do this, people will relate to you, and more importantly, they will want to do business with you afterwards.

How Can I Be More Relatable?

Visit PlatinumPresentationsBook.com to get additional resources Delatorro has created to help you maximize this content and take your presentations to the Platinum level.

Section 3:

After Your Next Presentation

If you like this book,
you will LOVE the Audio Companion Coaching Program
Over 4 Hour of Transformative Coaching from Delatorro on 5 Audio CDs

Visit www.PlatinumPresentationsBook.com to Order Today.

36. BE CLIMACTIC
Close Strong

Because of the way the human mind works, we tend to remember how things start and how they end – the middle gets a little convoluted unless you have killer speech organizational skills – which you should after reading and applying this book. My point is that people will remember how you started your presentation, key stories, powerful quotes/tweetables and how you end your presentation. It's vitally important that you close strong. Close on a high. Remember the overall purpose of your close is to button up all the content you promised them in the open in the body of your message. The Close is where you remind your audience of what you put in their filing cabinet drawer then nicely tuck the drawers back into their minds and hearts for good.

In addition, your close also needs to position your product, service or call-to-action as the primary next step for them to take. Now that we are at the conclusion, it's time for them to DO SOMETHING once they leave the room. Up until the Close, you were in charge. Once the Close happens, they are back in charge, and you quickly have less and less influence over their thoughts and actions. Your close needs to educate your audience on exactly what to do next. In your mind, replace the world close with commencement. I LOVE the word commencement because it has a double-meaning. While we are accustomed to commencement meaning the end of something (graduation from high school or college), it also means to START to BEGIN.

As you craft and deliver the close of your presentation remember that your close is actually a commencement. Its purpose is to end the presentation *and* to start the enrollment process. Enroll them into what? Whatever your Call to Action is. So close strong because a lot rides on your ability to do so.

How Can I Be More Climactic?

37. BE APPRECIATIVE
Thank The Audience And Here's Why

I know … I know …I know! I'm going against the grain on this one. There is so much teaching in the form of videos, articles, publications and so forth that espouse it's not professional or necessary to THANK your audience primarily because if you did a great job, your audience should be thanking you. And YES, that's true, yet here's why I believe you should thank your audience.

In 2018 and beyond, people's attention spans have gotten shorter and shorter. In fact, one study reported that people's attention span used to be 13 seconds, and now people's attention span has dwindled down to 8 seconds. If an audience gives you their attention for the length of your presentation and doesn't disengage or retreat to their mobile device or some other form of work – they deserve a Thank You. If your audience participated during your presentation and gave you good energy, laughed at your jokes and got quiet during your emotional moments – they deserve a Thank You. If they gave your good verbal and non-verbal feedback during your presentation, feedback that you used in the moment to create even more magical moments – they deserve a Thank You. If they arrived on time, got seated and put the rest of their lives on pause long enough to give you a true chance at changing their lives – they deserve a Thank You. We as communicators have to remember that a speech, presentation, message, gig, talk or whatever you want to call it, is still a co-created experience. You of course are a communicator, but so is your audience. It's their feedback and interaction that allows us to shine. So feel free to thank your audience for being a great audience. And if you don't think thanking a good audience is necessary, just wait till you have a few bad audiences and I promise you will change your tune.

Yes, you worked hard to deliver your wisdom, insight, knowledge, experience and principles to them that will make their lives better, but they did their part in receiving it well.

So again…THANK YOUR AUDIENCE!

How Can I Be More Appreciative?

_____

_____

_____

_____

_____

_____

_____

_____

_____

_____

_____

_____

_____

_____

38. BE APPROACHABLE
People Will Be Nervous About Meeting You

If you think your audience is impressed with you before you speak, just wait until afterwards. The fanfare quadruples once you've delivered on all the hype, the marketing and the branding. Once people see for themselves who you are and what you're about and they experienced the impact of your content and you've made them visualize how the implementation of said content will improve their family, faith, finances and future – people are going to be very wowed.

Simply remember a time when you were really excited to hear someone speak. Think back to how nervous you were to approach them beforehand to introduce yourself because you didn't want to interrupt their flow and their prep. Now, think of what it felt like to try to get their attention AFTER they were done and there was a mad dash to talk to them, ask questions, take photos, get resources or what have you. Do you remember? Well, that's how your audience will feel.

Be approachable. Smile. Shake hands. Genuinely say THANK YOU for all the compliments, accolades, applause and celebratory things people will say and ways in which they will say it. For example, I make it super easy for someone to approach me to take a photo. In fact, I say from the stage, "Listen, I can't wait to high-five you, hug your neck and take a selfie with you – so meet me in the foyer immediately after this presentation." By saying that in my close, I am inviting that interaction and showing that I am approachable and it's perfectly okay to come say Hello. Then, as people are approaching you, once they get close enough for you to read their nametag (if they have one), say "Hello, (name), wonderful to meet you, did you enjoy the presentation today? How can I serve you further?"

Be approachable and watch as your calendar and bank account fill up because your audience feels like you are just as nice off stage as you are on stage.

How Can I Be More Approachable?

_____

_____

_____

_____

_____

_____

_____

_____

_____

_____

_____

_____

_____

_____

39. BE VISIBLE
Stay In An HTA Where Your Audience Can See You And Engage With You

My friend, there is only one of you and hundreds of them. Once you get off that stage and people begin to swarm, it's hard for people to see you. It's very important that you be visible to your entire audience after your presentation. Decide in advance where you will situate yourself so that people can come to one central place, what I call HTA (High Traffic Area) to conduct post-event business with you.

You want this area to be easy to find - close to the entrance and exit and a place that people have to walk past. Scout out where the best place is and display your materials there. Also, make sure that you quickly get to your table immediately after you speak. Don't linger at the front of the room or the stage because wherever your audience sees you – is where they will begin to migrate. I've seen thousands of communicators lose business, opportunity, money, sales and leads all because they didn't get to their area of visibility quickly enough. Being visible sometimes also means that you need to come back to your table often. For example, if you speak in the morning and there is a 15 minute break after you speak, you may catch a good 60% of the people who do business with you –do it during that first break. If you leave right after the speech and immediate break, you've left 40% of your business unhandled because you were not visible.

A better strategy is to staff your table immediately after your presentation if in the morning, and then come back again and staff your table during lunch – an HTA time during most business meetings and events. I've doubled my sales, leads and opportunities just because I come back during the lunch break and finish doing business with the people that had to go to the restroom, had to go get their credit card or had to rush to another session during your first break. There are 100 reasons why people can't do business with you right away, so being visible by making a 2nd appearance is just smart!

How Can I Increase My Visibility?

40. BE FIRED UP
Remember You're Still ON

If you did your job correctly – hours, days and even weeks after you've walked off stage, your audience should remember the important elements of your presentation. In fact, immediately after your presentation your audience should be shaking your hand and interacting with you while their hearts and minds are in a time-warp because they are still thinking about all the feelings as if you're still on stage presenting. It's vitally important that you remember to remain in the same spirit and a similar energy-state to what you had on stage because in the view of your typical audience member, you *are* still on stage. They want a piece of who inspired, motivated, challenged, encouraged and persuaded them.

I've seen so many speakers and presenters miss out on tons of opportunities not because of a lack of a table or a lack of asking for business cards – but because of a lack of staying in the same energy as they had when they first captivated their audience. Be consistent to whatever being On means based on who you showed them you were on stage.

> If you were passionate & energetic on stage - model that at your table.
> If you were no-nonsense & brass tax on stage–model that at your table.
> If you were witty & punchy on stage – be that at your table.
> If you were coachy & solution-oriented on stage – be that at your table.

Get my point? It's like they say in relationships…whatever it took to hook your mate, it will take all of that to keep your mate. I can't tell you how many times I've been in the restroom after hearing a speaker speak and listening to talk about how that person was awesome on stage but mean, rude, short, distant, aloof or just different at their table. First it made them not want to invest with that speaker. Second it made them question the content. And what's worse, there's a third negative – they began to think all speakers are like this. Remember, BE ON for however long it takes to conduct after-stage business and watch your sales, referrals, leads, spinoff and future opportunities skyrocket.

How Can I Be More Fired Up?

_____

_____

_____

_____

_____

_____

_____

_____

_____

_____

_____

_____

_____

_____

_____

41. BE CONFIDENT
That The Resources You Have For Them
WILL Change Their Lives

Okay...this one is gonna hurt some of you. *Question:* Do you believe in the
solution you're selling? The reason I ask this powerful question is because I see
so *so* many communicators, speakers, authors, coaches and difference-makers
act super confident on stage but be barely confident at their tables afterwards. It
makes their sales and follow up results plummet through the floor. My friend,
your audience is going to be confident in your solution to the degree that YOU
are confident that it will help them. One of the BIGGEST things that I feel
affects your ability to be confident at your table is the amount of width and depth
- meat and potatoes - that you put into your material. Listen, I don't care what
your CTA (Call To Action) is, whatever it is, it needs to have substance or you
won't believe enough in it to convince people to ACT. Remember, in that
moment they – the audience – are not confident in your product. They have not
experienced it. What they are buying is the solution to the pain that they have –
based on the jumper cables of your confidence in that resource. Your confidence
gives them the temporary boost they need to pull out their wallets and conduct
business with you afterwards.

If you barely worked on your book – you won't feel confident selling it.
If you borrowed other people's work – you won't feel confident selling it.
If you plagiarized someone's ideas – you won't feel confident selling it.
If someone ghostwrote your book without your input – you won't feel confident selling it.
If your graphics look cheap and discounted – you won't feel confident selling it.

In other words, if you half-assed the process – you will FEEL like you are half-
assing people when you talk to them about your product. Buying is an emotional
process. People will be expecting to FEEL a certain level of confidence while
they are conducting business with you – and even after they leave your presence.

Be confident in your pricing.
Be confident in your content.
Be confident in what the website, the membership portal, the landing page will do.
Be confident in the process that your new customers will go through.
Be confident that what you are selling them will really work...if you are, it will show.

How Can I Be More Confident?

_____

_____

_____

_____

_____

_____

_____

_____

_____

_____

_____

_____

_____

_____

42. BE RESOURCEFUL
Show Them How Your Product Can Benefit Them

Show how your product can benefit them. This is an advanced technique, it will really create massive results if you do it correctly. Be a resource my friend. What I mean by that is while I do want you to be confident in your product or service benefiting your audience, I also want you to – at the exact same time – be a trusted advisor showing how your product is part of a total solution they need. It's a direct and an indirect way of encouraging them to grow overall. Be resourceful enough at your table to mention other elements of their solution; some having to do with your products and some that don't. Remember – people do business with people they know, like and trust.

Let me give you an example. Let's say that I am a health/wellness presenter and I want everyone in my audience to buy my nutritional cookbook that shows people how to cook healthier meals at home, save money, eat better, lose weight and spend more quality time with family. I would mention all those benefits from the stage –then, at my table while I am taking to a prospective buyer of my book, I would also say, "In addition to getting this book, you should go to your local Wholefoods store and buy some turmeric, some omega 3, 6 and 9s and a good probiotic. Adding these to your nutrition plan, along with following my recipes and two good cardiovascular walks each week will get you closer to your goal!"

Look what I just did. I put my resource, my CTA and my offering in with a 3-part solution for that customer. You can say this from the stage as well. Showing steps that you don't necessarily financially benefit from. We teach, model and make you practice sales scripts like this at my 3-day program called *Speaking Business Mastery* held 2 times per year. Be a resource and show your customer how your CTA is only part of a bigger solution. Turning them on to an additional book, event or idea makes them trust you 10x more- when trust is high – spending is high. Just saying…

How Can I Be More Resourceful?

_____

_____

_____

_____

_____

_____

_____

_____

_____

_____

_____

_____

_____

_____

_____

43. BE QUICK
Tons Of People Want To Talk To You
Take A Few Seconds With Each Person

This is yet another skill that truly takes time and practice with various types of audiences to truly master, but it's super important. You have to be quick as you interact with people. In this business of sharing information with audiences and then giving them a Call to Action – you don't have a lot of time. You will make money and lose money in seconds. This is ZERO exaggeration. You can make thousands and lose thousands of dollars in revenue and future opportunities in seconds depending upon the event – so you have to be quick as you interact with the population of people that want to engage with you after your presentation.

If you are a super-parent and speak at your local PTA and share 20 new ideas to get your kids off of tech & spending more time with family, completing their chores and cultivating a deeper spiritual connection – you are gonna have tons of those parents want to not just talk to you, but what? Talk to you about their specific kid, their personality style and which of the 20 ideas they think will work best for their kid. Which is awesome and great. But ...

You don't have the time at your table to adequately listen to each parent tell you this. You may want to, and it may be useful to hear, but you just don't have time. Let's run the numbers. If 100 parents are there and each has 2 kids that's a possible 200 stories you COULD hear at your table, but no one has time to hear all of that, and right after a speech is not the opportune time when 40% of those 100 want to buy your book and audio products that share all 50 of your parent hacks. How do you take care of 40 customers in 30 minutes? You need to greet them, get their contact info, process their payment, sign their book, and take a selfie in some instances all in about 45 seconds PER PERSON! You've got to be quick. You can't look through 10 photos in their phone and you can't coach them privately. I know you want to help them, but you can't and be fair to the others. Once you've conducted all immediate business, if there are still people waiting – then and only then do you invest more time. Based on this example, you gotta be quick because you have to do everything I mentioned in less than 45 seconds per customer.

How Can I Be Quicker?

44. BE CONSIDERATE
Of Other Speakers, Other Program Happenings And Other Event Happenings

The mark of a true amateur presenter is someone who shows no thought for the other programming dynamics involved in an event and only focuses on their presentation and audience. Your part of the conference, convention, event or seminar is just that – *part* of it. There are many other elements and aspects of it that must all come together, even if you are the Keynote speaker.

Packing up too slow could delay another speaker by 15 minutes.

Leaving your laptop plugged in after your talk could hinder another speaker's sound check.

Coaching a semi-circle of your raving fans is great, but doing so inside the room could draw attention away from the next speaker.

Going 20 minutes over on your breakout session time could cause a domino effect and throw off all the rest of the sessions that day.

Be considerate of what's happening right after you're done and make sure you take that into account as you function at your product table and conduct business after your presentation is over. You can give a great presentation but be very self-centered afterwards creating a bad reputation. Be awesome then take your business into the hallway so things can flow without interruption.

Also, keep your table participants quiet and respectful. I have said this from my table many times, "Ladies and gentleman, I can't wait to serve you however the conference has started back up, so please let's all be considerate and keep our voices down while we invest in our dreams and aspirations." And people appreciate that.

How Can I Be More Considerate?

_____

_____

_____

_____

_____

_____

_____

_____

_____

_____

_____

_____

_____

_____

_____

45. BE COACHABLE
Learn How You Could Have Made Your
Presentation Even Better

In 2016 I attended two different Tony Robbins events. They were both amazing. During the events I would text back and forth with several friends of mine who actually work for The Tony Robbins Organization. And after an amazing 4 or 5 days one of the most amazing things that I learned from my friends is that before Tony leaves an event to go to another city, he sits his team down to determine how he could make his event better. In other words, even though many people consider Tony the best, he and his team know that they can always improve.

What about you? Now that you've done a great job and touched many lives, as you leave the venue and are in your car or your flight heading home; ask yourself: How could I make that better?

How can I improve?
How can I tell that story a little better next time?
How can I incorporate that visual a little smoother next time?
How can I anticipate my audiences' question a litter better next time?
How can I work the crowd a little better next time?
How can I increase my closing ratio by 3% next time?
How can I explain the process for opting into my newsletter or joining my podcast?

All of these questions will help you with what the Japanese call *CANI*
C ontinuous
A nd
N ever-ending
I mprovement

Ask the meeting planner, the conference host, your staff, your team, your top students, your trusted inner circle and yourself how you can get better. Then LISTEN and apply it immediately then watch your next presentation be your best presentation. Be coachable enough to ask for and implement feedback.

How Can I Be More Coachable?

_____

_____

_____

_____

_____

_____

_____

_____

_____

_____

_____

_____

_____

_____

46. BE CELEBRATORY
Focus On Celebrating The Audience For The Difference Your Message Will Make In their Lives

One of the things I am most known for is this phrase, "I'm so excited for your next level! I can't wait for you to begin using X, Y or Z. Send me an email and let me know how this resource is impacting your life, business and/or family."

Now…why do I say this after all my presentations? Because it's TRUE. I really and truly am excited for the next level of the people in my audience. I actually care if they apply what I am teaching them. So … I tell them that.

And what's amazing is that many times it's my excitement *for* them that helps them make the buying decision to get physical resources, online resources or come work with me live. My friend, your audience will be drawn to you more and more when you are celebratory of their journey and evolution.

Another way to celebrate your audience as they approach you is to congratulate them on their current career up to this point and let them know that whatever change they seek to make – they CAN make it powerfully with your help and guidance. Congratulate them on where they have been and then get excited about where they are going.

Ever have a car battery go dead on you? Yeah, I know…it kinda sucks doesn't it?

Well, it never ceases to amaze me how quick the jumper cable process is. The car battery could have been dead for minutes, hours or even days. But one jump from a strong battery and that dead battery can begin to recharge itself. That's exactly what your confidence and belief in your audience members does for them. It gives them the jump they need in the moment to take them further.

Celebrate that.

How Can I Be Celebratory?

_____

_____

_____

_____

_____

_____

_____

_____

_____

_____

_____

_____

_____

_____

47. BE FRIENDLY
Nothing Will Kill Your Credibly Faster Than Being Personable On Stage And A Jerk Off Stage

I'll be honest with you. There are a lot of things that can go wrong during a presentation that can make you want to be not-so-friendly afterwards. Maybe you didn't eat first and you're starving. Maybe you developed a headache during your presentation and haven't had time to take something for it. Maybe you tried to break in a new pair of shoes and it's gonna take longer than you thought – so now your dogs are barking. Maybe you got a challenging text from a family member right before you went on stage, and a worse one once you got off stage. Maybe the content you presented didn't land exactly as you expected…

No jerks allowed during the events. There are a myriad of reasons why you could feel one way getting on the stage and a completely different way after getting off stage, but guess what????

The audience doesn't know and more importantly they don't care. Nothing will kill your credibility faster than being personable on stage and a jerk off stage.

They want you to be nice, friendly, sweet, approachable and pleasant when they come to visit with you.

Your argument with your spouse, your allergies, your less-than-ideal rental car – none of that matters to them. In that moment – they just want you to be sweet. So my friend, a part of speaking is acting –put on the face and be friendly because nothing will destroy the impact of your message more or the credibility of your content more than being one way on stage and changing and being mean, distant, stand-offish or rude off stage. Smile, wave, laugh and cater to your audience and they will respond by engaging with your offers, opting into your lead-generation platform and hopefully doing some form of next-step business with you.

How Can I Be Friendlier?

48. BE REFERABLE
Use Business Cards and Ask For People To Recommend You To Others While It's Fresh On Their Minds

Scripture reminds us that we have not, because we ask not. There are bigger doors that can be opened for you by the people that heard you speak but you've gotta ask for the business. You must ask for what you want and need. Many times we bring business cards to meetings but we don't ask people to take them. We put them on the table and allow people to take them at will. I want you to make it EASY for people to want to refer business to you. Ask people to pick up a few of your cards and give them out to people who are looking for the same type of learning experience that they just had.

The nanosecond you are done speaking, your audience shifts from an audience to hopefully a newly trained and motivated sales and marketing team. That's right. If you did your job correctly, that audience should be excited to go out and tell their following, family and friends the content you provided and the impact it had on their life. What benefit is this to you? Well, if properly equipped, this audience turned sales and marketing team can do much more than buy products and give your business cards out. A percentage of them can also refer you future business, connections and opportunities similar to if not bigger than the original door that allowed your paths to cross in the beginning.

I say it all the time, a referral is the best product sale. Another engagement or a spin-off piece of business is always the best way that your audience can thank you for the impact you made on them. They can help you by helping you do it again – just bigger, better and badder.

Ask your audience and your table traffic to refer business to you and use business cards, promotional products, brochures or whatever you have to equip them with what they need to sell you.

How Can I Be More Referable?

_____

_____

_____

_____

_____

_____

_____

_____

_____

_____

_____

_____

_____

_____

49. BE GONE
Your Value Increases In The Minds Of People When They Know You're Not Overly Accessible

Okay ... let's go there. This one may not be popular but it's true.

Here's my suggestion. I think you should speak and give 150% of your best and then stay afterwards for a brief amount of time to conduct business and then after a while I suggest that you leave. That's right. Be Gone. Your value increases when you're not overly accessible.

Here's the reason why. Your value goes UP in people's minds when they realize that your free time is in short supply. People will respect your time more when they know that you won't be around for long. Why do people get speeding tickets on the way to the airport? Because the airlines have trained us that they will leave if we are not on time. So we hurry up, sometimes just to wait for delays, right? My point is that how long you stay after your event, speech, gig or presentation tells the audience how valuable your time is to you. And many people will take up large amounts of your time for no reason – *if you let them.*

People will act if you create urgency, but if you don't create urgency people will drag their feet and I'm sorry my friend, but you've got better things to do with your time than sit around staffing your table while you wait for your next trickled sale. Tell people you will only be there for 20 minutes after the presentation. When people come up to you and ask if you will be there long enough for them to run to their car or back to their hotel room, say, "If you hurry, I won't leave if I see you are back before I have to go...now go and come right back!" Guess what...they do!

Create genuine urgency and it will happen. Without it, you could be twiddling your thumbs for a long time.

How Can I Be Gone?

50. BE COMPLIMENTARY
Of The Host Of The Meeting And Tell Them What You Enjoyed About Their Event

This one is super important! If you want to get invited back you should make it very easy for the host or meeting planner to WANT to have you back by letting them know how much you appreciate all the work that went into pulling off the entire event – of which your speech or presentation was simply a part. While it was an EPIC part – if you did your job right and crushed the stage – it was still only one part of a multi-part process with many layers. Most events, meetings, conferences and conventions take months if not even years to plan and execute. Your presentation lasted for an hour, half-day or maybe even full-day. Regardless, the actual amount of delivery time that you had on stage pales in comparison to the amount of work it took to pull off the entire event. So give credit to whom credit is due. Give honor to whom honor is due.

Take some time and pull the event host aside to sincerely let them know how honored you were to be a part of the program and tell them several things you enjoyed about the event... that have NOTHING TO DO with your presentation.

This is so important. For example, tell them you loved the venue they selected, or tell them how you thought the food was, or how much you liked the graphics and the conference theme. Compliment their staff and team and production company for the job they did. These compliments from a Keynote speaker go a much longer way than you can imagine and even if you're not the Keynote, just someone coming back and pulling them aside to compliment versus complain will mean the world to them. I know because I not only speak, but I also HOST events so I know all the headaches that go into being on the planning side.

Take time before you leave to compliment the host and your feedback will go a long way towards making them feel valued and appreciated and also potentially helping you be remembered and invited back in the future.

How Can I Be More Complimentary?

_____

_____

_____

_____

_____

_____

_____

_____

_____

_____

_____

_____

_____

_____

_____

_____

_____

51. BE SOCIAL
Share On Social Media The Impact Of The Event And Encourage Others To Attend The Next One

If Social Media matters to your client, it should matter to you. Share the impact of the event and encourage others to attend the next one.

> ➤ Was there a conference hashtag? Did you use it in your presentation?
> ➤ Did people follow up as a result of your presentation?
> ➤ Did people retweet your quotable moments?
> ➤ Did the client offer a contest for a socially sharing audience member?
> ➤ Was there a photo contest?

These are all things that may not mean much to you…but they mean a great deal to your client because all of these are aspects and elements of the conference that were built-in that required their time and attention. If you got new social media followers as a result of their audience, their marketing and their event – even though it was your presentation – you should still at least participate a little and post a message, share a photo or at least favorite, like, or heart a few comments that relate to your message. Answer a few questions that people post inside the attendee FB page for instance. Maybe during your Uber ride back home or to the airport or to the train station or however you get back home, you dedicate just 5 minutes to investigate the social media title wave that took place AFTER you spoke. Your client will greatly appreciate that you took the time to engage online after it was all over and even share on your page how great of an event you just participated in because that's free marketing of their event.

Take a few moments after your presentation and comment on the FB page for the event, tweet a few people who took the most twitter notes, accept the 20 new people that requested to be your connection on Linked In and like a few posts that you see people make about your presentation or the event overall.

It goes a much longer way than you think.

How Can I Be More Social?

_____

_____

_____

_____

_____

_____

_____

_____

_____

_____

_____

_____

_____

_____

_____

_____

52. BE STICKY
Follow Up With The Client Afterward And Strike While The Iron Is Hot

Jim Rohn the great business philosopher has said this many *many* times…
> The Fortunes are in the Follow Up.
> The Fortunes are in the Follow Up.
> The Fortunes are in the Follow Up.

People get busy & distracted FAST! People get side-tracked & lose focus quickly.

If you give a great presentation and Crush The Stage, people should come up to you asking about ways to book you for other groups. If that is not happening, then you need to come see me and allow me to work with you LIVE at Crush The Stage for 3 Life-changing days. Learn more at www.CrushTheStageLive.com.

Once this happens and people rush to want to do business with you again – no matter how well-meaning these people are –THEY WILL FORGET ABOUT BOOKING YOU! They will get busy, distracted and side-tracked with other things right in front of their face and your next paid gig is not a priority. Growing your branding is never *their* daily focus. Building your business is not something they wake up adding to their To Do list. Sooo, you must follow up. It's been said that 7 touches AFTER an encounter with a product or service equals a sale. Sometimes it takes a customer 7 different after-the-fact touches to ACT and most of us give up after 1 or 2 touches. That means email, text, call, email again, message, email a 3rd time and call again. It's tedious–learn ways to automate much of this process with technology but make no mistake my friend – the fortunes are in the follow up. Sticky means TOP OF MIND! Remember to reach out quickly after you've impacted them and ask for referrals, testimonials and follow colleague contact info immediately after you've made an impression. This is important to get your client on FIRE for YOU right after the event and the first few days or weeks after you've done a great job. You wait a month or more and … The thrill is gone …
> Follow up often and strike while the iron is *HOT!*

How Can I Be Stickier?

_____

_____

_____

_____

_____

_____

_____

_____

_____

_____

_____

_____

_____

_____

_____

_____

AFTERWORD

Mega Mega Mega CONGRATULATIONS my friend!

Wow. You did it! It has been reported that 70% of people never read a book from cover to cover so if you are reading this...you are a High Achiever and a Finisher and I like that about you.

Sooooooo????? What did you think?

Did you enjoy Platinum Presentations?

What was your favorite part about this book?

_____

_____

_____

_____

_____

_____

Of the 52 Tips that I shared with you, list your Top 10 to Implement NOW!

_____

_____

_____

_____

_____

Very nice. I like to see actionable takeaways.

So WHAT'S NEXT?   Great Question.

Now that you have learned from me in book form, let's take it to the next level so you can learn from me online and LIVE! Sound good? If I were you and I got great value from a book like this, these would be my best next steps.

1. Join or increase your hustle in a strong, competitive Toastmasters Club and apply everything I have taught you each week as you compete. Visit www.ToastmasterToTopSpeaker.com to get Top Speaker Advantage pack.

2. Join www.CrushTheStageUniversity.com and begin the Online Mentoring Program with Delatorro.

3. Visit www.CrushTheStageLive.com and see when Delatorro is hosting the next 3-Day Live Training and ENROLL immediately.

4. Watch for FREE the 1st Season of THE KEYNOTE – Delatorro's Inspirational Business Reality TV Show at www.TheKeynoteTVShow.com

My friend, you've GOT THIS! I sincerely hope and pray that you got massive value from this book and I hope that it's just the beginning of a long and successful transformation in your life and career.

Here's to many years of you delivering Platinum Presentations,

Delatorro